CAN YOU SEE WHAT I SEE?
NATURE

READ-AND-SEEK LEVEL 1

WALTER WICK

Cartwheel B·O·O·K·S ® SCHOLASTIC INC.

New York Toronto London Auckland Sydney
Mexico City New Delhi Hong Kong Buenos Aires

Text copyright © 2008 by Walter Wick.
"Animal Kingdom," "Washed Ashore," "Fall Finds," and "Dino Diorama" from *Can You See What I See? Cool Collections* © 2004 by Walter Wick; "Happy Christmas to All" and "Down the Chimney" from *Can You See What I See? The Night Before Christmas* © 2005 by Walter Wick; "Spring Things" from *Can You See What I See? Cool Collections* © 2006 by Walter Wick; "Beauty & the Beast," "The Little Mermaid," and "Hansel & Gretel" from *Can You See What I See? Once Upon a Time* © 2006 by Walter Wick.

Library of Congress Cataloging-in-Publication Data
Wick, Walter.
Can you see what I see? : nature read-and-seek / Walter Wick.
p. cm.
ISBN 0-439-86226-4
1. Picture puzzles–Juvenile literature. I. Title. II. Title: Nature read-and-seek.
GV1507.P47W5133 2008
793.73–dc22   2007020321

ISBN-13: 978-0-439-86226-4
ISBN-10: 0-439-86226-4

10 9 8 7 6 5 4 3 2 1   8 9 10 11 12/0

Printed in the U.S.A. • First printing, January 2008

Dear Reader,

Read the words and find the hidden objects. For an extra challenge, cover the picture clues at the bottom of each page with your hand.

Have fun!

Walter Wick

Can you see

a snail,

a frog,

and 2 eggs?

Can you see

3 pigs

and an elephant

on 2 legs?

Can you see

a water lily,

2 monkeys,

a duck?

Can you see

a ladybug,

2 starfish,

a truck?

Can you see

a shark,

a bottle,

a pail?

Can you see

a deer,

a broom,

and a nail?

Can you see

a feather,

an ant,

and a ring?

Can you see

3 acorns,

a bee,

and red string?

Can you see

2 snakes,

an egg,

and a shell?

Can you see

a horse,

a bear,

and a bell?

Can you see

a bird,

a hat,

and a fox?

Can you see

a rabbit,

2 birds,

and a box?

acorn

ant

box

bear

bee

bell

bird

bottle

broom

deer

duck

egg

elephant

feather

fox

frog

hat

horse

ladybug

monkey

nail

pail

pig

rabbit

ring

shark

shell

snake

starfish

string

truck

water lily

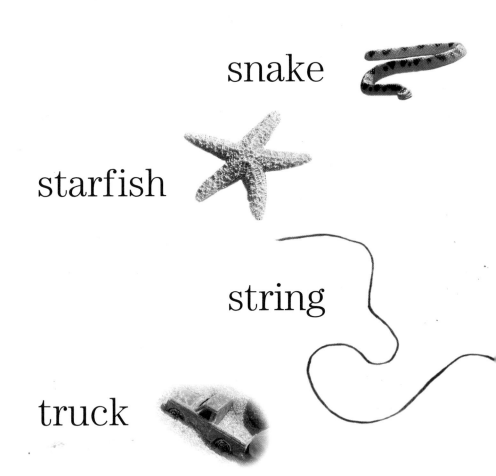